~SOMETHING TO THINK ABOUT~

THE WORLD IS A HYPOCRITE

SOMETHING TO THINK ABOUT, THE WORLD IS A HYPOCRITE by: CHIEF SINNA

www.somethingtothinkabout.life

Published by:
©2023
VJ PUBLISHINGHOUSE, LLC. 20451 NW 2nd Avenue
Suite112 Miami Gardens, Fl. 33169
www.vjpublishinghouse.com

Formatted for publishing by VENTURE22
www.venture22.io

ISBN#: 978-1-939236-15-9 (Paperback) PRINTED IN THE UNITED STATES OF AMERICA. THIS BOOK IS PRINTED ON ACID-FREE PAPER.

IN LOVING MEMORY OF

"GRANNY"

~DEDICATION~

MOST IMPORTANTLY, I WOULD LIKE TO FIRST START BY SAYING THAT NONE OF THIS WOULD BE POSSIBLE WITHOUT GOD HAVING DEEMED IT SO. WITHOUT FURTHER ADO, I WANT TO THANK GOD FOR BLESSING ME TO BE BORN TO THE MOTHER OF MY MOTHER, WHO'S THE GREATEST TEACHER OTHER THAN THE CREATOR'S SON THAT I KNOW. I KNOW MANY PEOPLE TALK ABOUT HOW SPECIAL THEIR GRANDMOTHER WAS AND IS TO THEM, BUT THIS SPIRITUAL BEING OF A LADY WAS SOMETHING SPECIAL. SHE'S THE REASON WHY I HAVE THE UNDERSTANDING OF WHAT UNDERSTANDING MEANS. I REMEMBER TELLING HER THAT THE BOOK WOULD BE CALLED, "THE WORLD IS A HYPOCRITE," AND SHE SAID NO BABY, CALL IT "SOMETHING TO THINK ABOUT"

AND MAKE THE WORLD IS A HYPOCRITE THE SUBTITLE. INSTEAD OF A ROLE MODEL, SHE'S THE LIFE MODEL THAT GOD PLACED IN MY LIFE TO SET ME ON THE PATH THAT GOD HAS ME ON THIS DAY. I THANK YOU FOR THAT ALWAYS. AND TO ALL THE NEGATIVITY THAT'S EVER COME MY WAY, I THANK YOU BECAUSE IT FUELED ME. TO ALL THAT BELIEVED IN ME, I THANK YOU AS WELL. I DEFINITELY WOULD LIKE TO THANK MY CHILDREN FOR THEM BEING A LIFE FORCE OF HOPE. THANK YOU, L.C.K.T.R.M.PJ.

~TABLE OF CONTENTS~

~FORWARD~

By: Chief Sinna

When I was eight years old, something extraordinary happened to me. I was tackled to the ground during a football game in a neighbor's backyard. When I looked up and squinted in the sunlight, I saw the Creator Son shaped in the form of clouds holding a rod. He was big as a skyscraper, and as real as I am alive today.

He pointed to me and said, "In time, all will be right." I was dazed and proceeded to tell my friends, asking if they saw Him too. They said I was crazy and laughed at me. I was so frightened that I ran home to tell my Grandmother that I saw Him.

She said, "I know you did, baby." She's the only person who knows me to my core and believes in my experiences with Him.

When I was 20 years old, it happened again when stationed in Israel on a Navy ship. I went overboard and had an out-of-body experience when I was submerged in the ocean. It was more like a dream, as if I was unconscious.

God spoke to me this time and asked, "How long will you ignore me, Chief Sinna?"

I remember wondering why God had allowed me to live because, at that moment, I truly hated myself due to the sinful things I had done, which I will explain later in this book.

Fast forward to many years later on June 26th, 2011, at 10:48 am, when I was 36 years old and baptized for the first time. I remember what happened like it was yesterday. When I was dipped into the water by the Pastor, I had another out-of-body experience. I was above the lake and saw at least 200 people. This time when God came to me, I chose a different reaction. Instead of denying and forgetting about His message, I wanted to understand Him. From that moment on, God was in charge of my life and had a plan for me. Part of my mission was to send me forward with His message to reach all of you. I was supposed to use my experiences to enlighten you about the mistakes I've made to help you avoid making those same mistakes. I was also to treat all people with kindness, including myself.

After I got baptized, my Grandmother told me she was proud of me. I remember saying, "Granny, you've never told me that before?" And, she then said, "Boy, I ain't never had a reason to be proud of you until now."

Three months had passed, and on September 26th, 2011, at 10:48 pm, I was across the street from my house and on the phone with my Granny, who lives in Arkansas. I told her I believed my Great Grandmother wanted me to help bring the family together to have a family reunion like the one we had back in 1985.

My Granny said, "Baby, maybe she does." I also remember telling her that I saw a light in the sky, to which she replied, "Baby, that's nothing but an airplane." Keep in mind my Grandmother was in Arkansas while I was in Maple Grove, Minnesota, so she couldn't see what I was looking at unless she went outside and looked up in the sky. I kept saying, "No, Granny, that's not an airplane, that's something different."

All I know is that the light kept getting brighter and closer while I was on my cell phone with her. It mirrored the light John Travolta saw in the movie Phenomenon. Suddenly, for three seconds, it blinded me. That's when I ran back towards the house, away from it.

Then something miraculous happened, something I never envisioned myself doing. I fell to the ground and started yelling to God, "I'm sorry for being so selfish. Please forgive me for being greedy and doing all those sinful things. Tell me what to do?" While this was happening, I forgot about my Grandmother, who was still on the phone. She was yelling into the phone, "Boy, shut up and go read about Saul on the road to Damascus."

You see, Saul was the Chief of all sinners, and Damascus was a city in the middle east. My life mirrored Saul's life; he was on the road to righteousness.

I hung up the phone and cried hysterically because I finally understood what this profound experience of meeting God meant. He wanted me to take my experiences in my past and use them for the good of the people, those who couldn't help themselves. I was so scared that I ran into the house and asked my former wife and friends if they saw the same light. They weren't as lucky as I was. Later that night, I had the most bizarre dream. God came to me, and we had a conversation. He asked, "Chief Sinnar, do you know the root of all evil?" "Yes, it's the love of money." Then he said, "I know something you love more than money itself." "What is that?" He said, "Getting into the Gates of Heaven." I said, "I thought you wrote in the Bible that if we believe that your Son died on the cross for our sins, we'll be forgiven and granted eternal life." God replied, "You are right, but that applies to every man on earth except for you. Since you used to love money more than mankind, I want you to be the one for my mission."

God further explained that I would be put into a position of power, helping my company to become a billion-dollar company. When this happened, He said I needed to give the company away immediately. Then He said obedience was better than sacrifice and that if I were obedient and followed His word, I would make it into the Gates of Heaven.

He also said, "Rocks may get in your way, but your path shall remain straight and not the same." I was told my life would be sacrificed to help others without asking for anything. God told me that when I felt a chill, I was supposed to act upon whatever was taking place. I was to ignore what was happening if I didn't get a chill. To maintain my sanity, I needed to see a doctor to ensure I didn't have a brain tumor or other medical condition. The doctors told me I was as healthy as an ox. You'd have to hear more of my story to understand how I'm being used as God's instrument.

I can't make anyone believe me because I can't guarantee that I will wake up in the morning. No one is in control of what happens to us except for God. But I can tell you my story in hopes that you will choose to do the right thing based on the messages I've been given and share with you.

At a very young age, I learned the Bible, and I can still remember Matthew 17:20, which says, "If you have the faith of the grain of a mustard seed, you can move mountains."

We all have been given a choice to do great things, but not all of us have chosen that path. We can choose to ignore, but we can also choose to believe. I chose to believe, and I'll tell you why if you also choose to believe and walk with me through my journey. I promise to enlighten you.

~NOTES~

~CHAPTER 1~

F.A.I.T.H.

"FEELING. ALL. IMPOSSIBLE. THINGS. HAPPEN."

What is faith? We can't see it, but we know it's there. It's not a religious way of thinking; it's a spiritual way of thinking.

Faith is believing something because we sense and feel it to be true. Sometimes, we believe in faith automatically without thinking about it. For example, we have faith in oxygen because we breathe it. The same thing is true about the wind. We can't see it, but we can feel it. When someone says, 'I love you,' we believe they love us because we trust that person. When I got married, I didn't doubt that my wife would be unfaithful. When a child learns to ride a bike for the first time, parents have faith through prayer that their child is safe and doesn't fall. These are examples of how faith works when things are unseen and unknown. You can find confidence in people who believe in faith. All of us who take the chance and apply this simple feat in our way of thinking are the most successful people on this planet. They are the ones who keep going when others continue to believe they can't do something. My story dates back to when I was eight years old, and I believed the spirit of our Creator was living inside me. At this time, I used faith for personal gain rather than giving to others who were less fortunate. Once I understood what faith was and how it could benefit me, which meant there wasn't room for doubt, I used it to get all the money I ever wanted. Faith is powerful once we learn how to understand it and how it can be used in good and bad situations.

I believe F.A.I.T.H. is "Feeling. All. Impossible. Things. Happen." Being led to do something of which we're unsure is the true definition of what it means to have faith. Is it possible to have faith and doubt faith at the same time? Why would we want to doubt it if it's part of a belief system? Would you want someone to believe or trust in you? If your answer is yes, then you're asking simply for that person to have faith in you. Life is really simple; we choose to make it hard.

We only question the true meaning of faith when it's brought to our attention. As soon as we're aware that we're utilizing faith, we tend to allow doubt to get in our way, and that's when we can't achieve what we seek. We need to practice believing in faith. Let's take an example of sports. How do athletes know they'll make the team? Actually, they hope to make a specific team. I'm no scholar, but having hope is the same as having faith. With practice, we will be better at understanding it and learn to believe in faith.

What harm is there in having faith? When we choose to have faith, it's not supposed to harm us mentally, physically, financially, or spiritually. So why would anyone oppose applying faith to their everyday life when it can be beneficial? I remember growing up as a child and believing that I could do anything as long as I believed in God. My friends and family believed in me. I also wanted to be like Sam Walton, owner of Walmart, because we're both from Arkansas, and we are persistent, consistent, determined, and focused. Do you think Sam doubted what was in his heart? I don't think he did because he was able to move forward in creating Walmart because he believed in himself.

Based on being a messenger from God, it's my opinion that there's not one single person in this world who doesn't possess faith. In addition to having and believing in faith, there is also the kind of faith we have when we choose to believe in a higher power in the religious sense. We use words associated with faith such as belief, hope, certainty, and truth.

None of those words should hold doubt because they have the power to be positive. Looking at those words, I'm allowing the keyboard to architect my mind and finger strokes. Faith is also associated with the word 'can.' Sometimes, we find ourselves saying "we can do something." What would you call knowing we can do something without ever doing it? How about that athlete who stands at the free throw line shooting the basketball for the game-winner?

What do you think is going through his mind? Do you think he had doubts, or was he saying,' I hope I can make this free throw?' There are many scenarios where we apply faith and pair it with action without being mindful. I want to tell you about how I learned to have faith. It's not like we don't have it, we just don't always acknowledge or use it to the best of our ability. The only difference between you and me is that I choose to apply it to my life. I'll tell you a story. When I was 32 years old, I needed some things to change in my life, and I remember my Grandmother telling me to go to God's store, which was a real place in my mind. She said I didn't need to worry about paying for what I asked for because it was free. She enlightened me saying I could go there for anything, so I went and grabbed a bit of faith and asked for it to be strengthened. Little did I know, it was revealed I already had it.

The problem was that I always allowed doubt to come into my mind. When we learn to have faith and allow the Creator to take control of our life, we can do some of the greatest things mankind has ever seen. I was able to take faith with me during significant times in my life. For example, I was bullied physically and emotionally numerous times, starting at age 5. I prayed that I could figure out a way to prevent it, but the bullying continued. But I never gave up on trying to find a way to stop the bullying. I knew I was a nerd in school, and most of the guys who were into sports weren't as bright as I was, or they chose not to use their smarts.

Throughout that period, I learned that one of the athletes, who was one of the guys who bullied me, would be kicked off the team if he didn't improve his grades. One day I approached him and told him how I could make our situation a win-win for both of us. I proposed that if I helped him to maintain passing grades, not only was he to stop bullying me. he also was to make sure that other people didn't bully me because if they did, I wouldn't be in a position to help him with his grades, which would mean that he couldn't play ball, and his parents would be upset. Surprisingly, he agreed to my plan. You might be asking yourself how faith is displayed in this scenario. First, I prayed about it.

You see, nothing in life is guaranteed, but we hope for the best, and that's exactly what I did. Secondly, I identified the problem. Next, I isolated the problem, which then led me to overcome the problem. By pinpointing my thoughts, it accomplished the results I was hoping for. I can recall having faith many other times while growing up as a child.

Have you ever found yourself in a situation hoping that nobody would catch you doing something wrong? I'm sure I'm not the only one who had that first kiss from a girl or boyfriend while hoping that nobody catches you.

You see, without paying attention, we can have faith. It's something that happens naturally without having to be aware of it. Imagine how this world would be if we all channeled faith positively to overcome negative things happening in our world. Now, that would be so remarkable!

I voted for the first time when I was 18 years old. Bill Clinton, the Governor of Arkansas, was running for President. I knew what it was like to have him run our state, and I was hoping he would become the President of The United States. Did I know for sure that he would win?

No. Because I hoped he would win, I had to vote to demonstrate my faith.
At that tender age, straight out of high school, I enlisted in boot camp in the U.S. Navy. I remember waiting to get into the company. The uncertainty with waiting was that all the people who came before us were much more experienced in marching and how they carried themselves. None of us knew how to march, but that didn't discourage me. I hated how we were the laughingstock of the base because of our inexperience. Rather than feeling sorry for myself, I took the initiative and gathered a group of guys in my same position and asked them if they wanted to learn how to march so we wouldn't be laughed at anymore.

I knew this wasn't an impossible mission because I believed we could do this together. We could change how we felt about ourselves when we put the work in. The result was that we got better and weren't the base's laughingstock anymore. Following this experience, I was surprised to find out that someone was paying attention to what I was doing.

One day a commander walked up to me and asked who told me to take charge of the other recruits, and I said no one. I told him I needed to change how people looked at us. He told me that even though I was the smallest one in our company, he was impressed with my leadership skills, including my ability to believe, which resulted in him offering me the leadership position at boot camp C018. We can ask ourselves why the people in my company from all over the world followed this little guy from Arkansas. When it was all said and done, the answer that resonated among them was that they believed in me. The other recruits also had faith in themselves that they could change their thinking by doing the work, resulting in getting what they sought. You see, it's like a deadly deed without having and acting upon faith. There's much power and positivity when we apply faith to our way of thinking, feeling, and speaking.

In 1998, I was 23 years old when I left the Navy. I started working for a company called Peak Performance which sold environmental cleaning systems. I was tossed into the position of being a salesman. I had yet to gain experience in sales. My job-related experience only included cooking meals as I was a Chef in the Navy. For the first three months as a salesman, my colleagues made loads of money weekly, except for me. I doubted myself every day, partly because I was shy but also because I wasn't making any money. I hadn't made a single penny in sales. But, I had the belief that winners never quit, and quitters never won. With this belief in mind, I eliminated the doubt that I couldn't be the best salesman in the region.

Six months after I was hired, there was a contest for whoever sold the most units and earned the most money would have the chance to go to the Super-Bowl. I believed wholeheartedly, without a shadow of doubt that I could be that prize salesman. I ended up selling 11 units of environmental cleaning systems at $2,000 each and earned the title "Top Salesman" in the division. From then on, I made a total of $4,400 every month. I just knew that great things came for me whenever I had faith. There was no room for doubt. I trained my mind to believe that I would sell many units even though I started the position with doubt. Eventually, I became so great at my job that they gave me my own training class and with my help, the company became number 1 in the division of 4 states. As the above examples portray, when I believed in something I wanted, I had faith which did great things for me. When this happened, there wasn't anything I couldn't accomplish.

This is why I felt like I didn't need God earlier in my life. My mountain back then was what I wanted but didn't have. I'm not saying that just because you believe things will happen. I'm living proof that it takes work and faith to accomplish anything. We all have faith whether we choose to acknowledge it or not. Every second of every day, there are many examples of how faith is used in our lives. We must hope that we have another day to make a change. Faith can move any mountain, stumbling block, or rock that's in our way if we put forth the effort and allow ourselves to do what we need to do which is to PROGRESS.

The purpose of this entire first chapter is to tell you that we can have faith and that even though we have faith, we don't always act on it. If I can get you to change your way of thinking and to believe in yourself, then miraculous things can happen in your life, as they did in mine. I can't do anything alone unless God allows me to breathe and be able to do the work that He needs me to do. I have faith in you, hoping that you will heed to what I'm saying and believe it will change you, even in a minor way, because changing your way of THINKING, BELIEVING, and DOING will move mountains. F.A.I.T.H.

~DEEPEST THOUGHTS~

1. What areas of your life have there been things which gave you doubt that backed you up into a corner to force you to demonstrate faith?

2. What did you benefit by having doubt in your way of thinking?

3. Where in the chapter of faith after reading it, could you relate to your own experiences?

~NOTES~

~CHAPTER 2~

'FAVOUR'

For this book, I'll use the word favour which means the same thing as favor. That is, using our talents and time to do something for someone else. Because I'm a spiritual person, I opt to use the spelling favour like it is mirrored in the Bible. When a person shows favour they are providing a service for someone. Is it fair to say favour has the same value as currency?

Was there a time when you asked someone to do a favour for you? There are many ways we can discuss favour, but I'd like to discuss it as something valuable. What if we as a whole could substitute a favour in place of money? Would it still have the same effect? If we look at it from that perspective, then money and favour are equal. If Oprah Winfrey or any other high-net-worth individual gives someone a favour, will something good happen? Let's say we need something but have no money. All we have of value is our expertise and time.

Let's go back in time to when I was 13 years old and had to chop cotton for a living during the summer to help earn money for my family. The ironic thing about this was that I was born in the 70's. Slavery was well over, but that way of life still existed. My Granny made me get up at 5:00 am on the weekends, grab a gardening tool and wait to be picked up by the boss man to hit the fields. Remember, this was in Arkansas during the summer, and mosquito season was prevalent, not to mention the 100+degree weather.

I had to wear long sleeve shirts, long pants, and boots to protect my body from the mosquitos and my feet from snake bites. The boss was a white man who regularly said, "get out there and get those cucka bugs and morning glories." We had limited breaks because if we wanted to get paid, we had to be in the field all day. What's wrong with this picture from my point of view? Well, after working 14-hour days, I was paid $25 per day. I had to give my boss five dollars for the ride to and from the fields. It was hard work, and I wasn't allowed to keep the money. Instead, I had to give the money to my Granny, which went towards our household necessities.

Being a nerd growing up, one may think that I would use common sense when it came to earning money. I had none. I am still trying to figure out what to do with my earnings. Saving or investing money was never something that was taught to me. Simply, all I wanted was to keep the money that I had worked hard for.

Fast forward a few years to when I was 16 years old. I traveled to Dodge City, Kansas, and Sioux Falls, South Dakota. My main reason for doing this was to earn money to buy clothes for school. For six summers during break, I was sent off to babysit my aunt's and uncle's children. Even though I babysat these kids and earned my own money, my relatives used my money to buy clothes for me. This wasn't fair. Why couldn't I choose the things that I wanted? I knew then that money had power. It's the controller, and who controls it, if used correctly is what I wanted. I wanted it to do whatever I wanted, because money had power.

When I was 18, I graduated from high school and worked for Kentucky Fried Chicken. The green bug (money) had bitten me, and it was contagious! I remember what it was like to get that first paycheck. I threw out all my morals and values because money finally belonged to me and I could spend it on whatever I wanted. I was totally hooked on money by then.

I enrolled at Henderson State University in Arkansas as a freshman that same year. A man approached me and asked if I wanted to enter the Navy. Without really thinking, I signed the papers enlisting myself in the Navy. All I knew was that my tail was shipped off to boot camp before I knew it. When I was 19 years old, I returned to the United States.

While in the Navy, I spent time overseas on a Mediterranean Cruise on the supply ship of the U.S.S. Shenandoah AD 44. I had no idea what to expect but my shipmates told me I could earn and save a lot of money. I earned $1600 dollars per month. All I needed was $100 per month for living necessities for six months. Since I was in the Navy, my room, board, and meals were paid for. I went to the bank to see how much money I had earned and saved in the Navy. To my surprise, I had over $16,000 in my bank account. I was like a kid in a candy store. I thought I was rich! It was during this time that my love for money worsened. All of my teachings about money from the Bible flew out the window. I didn't need the Bible or God because I had a lot of money, and with money came power! My addiction to money was downright ruthless.

What happened here forward, no one could change, except for me. Boy, was I in for a rude awakening. I financed a new car. I was shopping as if I had all the money in the world. I was getting the much-needed attention that I had missed as a child. I rented a place with my cousin. I wasn't the laughingstock anymore like I used to be in the South. I was finally a man living in the now and didn't think my money could ever run out. But like the life cycle, all good things come to an end and eventually, it runs out. I didn't know what to do. I hadn't invested any of my money. I hadn't sent any money home to help my family. All I knew was that I had to find a way to get more of it. I couldn't steal or sell drugs because of the ramifications. I wondered how I would get money for the things I loved so much. For example, I wanted to have the newest fashion items, because those materialistic items made me feel very important. I simply loved money. One day out of nowhere, the answer struck me like a lightning bolt. I remembered my teachings from the Bible and recalled what my Granny told me when I was a child. The teachings I found in the Bible (KJV) in Proverbs 3:1-3:4 were the answers I was looking for.

Verse 1., "My son forget not my law; but let thine heart keep my commandments: 2. For length of days, and long life, and peace, shall they add to thee. 3. Let not mercy and truth forsake thee: bind them about thy neck; write them upon the tablet of thine heart: 4. So shalt thou find favour and good understanding in the sight of God and man" (KJV) 1961, p. 642. I was to be obedient to the instructions that were given to me. As long as I do that, I will have a prosperous life that will be prolonged.

I was to keep those instructions in my heart as if my life depended on them. If I were obedient, then favour would always be there when I needed it the most. I prayed for favour believing I would be granted the desires of my heart and that God wouldn't let me down. I had faith in the size of a grain of a mustard seed and found new ways to get more money. I remember my Granny's saying from Matthew 7:7, "Ask. Seek. Knock" (KJV) 1961, p. 6. So, that's what I did. I started asking for the things I wanted. I didn't know that I was obsessed with what money could do for me. I had to ensure I got what I desired, like attention, materialistic items, gorgeous women, and anything else I wanted. However, as soon as I got the money, I spent it. I constantly had to provide a service to get the money to get the things I wanted.

For example, my services consisted of whatever it was that I needed. When I needed a car, I sold enough cars to get my own. I would refer to enough people to buy jewelry from that particular store if it was jewelry. With the gift of gab, I even sold my spoken words to those who enjoyed and desired it. However, as time passed and I got older, the more I understood money, I realized its true value. It had none.

Between 1998-2005, when I was 23-30 years old, I had an accumulative amount of $7.8 million, which I had earned and saved from my various jobs and kept to myself. Throughout these years, I have always sought attention from others. The countless times I had been bullied throughout my life, no one liked me, so I was desperate for people to like me. I believed if I had money, they would like and accept me. Soon after, I was hanging out with the wrong crowd who took advantage of me because I was so rich.

Spending time with this bad crowd led me to be in a position where I couldn't work for a company. Instead, I had to work for myself. This is where learning to work for favour came into play. For years prior, I failed to notice that I was providing a service. I had the gift of connecting with people.

I was told I was great at marketing, advertising, and networking. I used faith to accomplish what I wanted. I was mindful that I had a gift to convince others. I could do anything that I put my mind to. Truth be told, it wasn't money I was seeking, it was what the money could do for me when I exchanged it for a favour. It was then that I applied faith to use my talents for people, and in return, I was given a favour. For example, if I wanted to attend an exclusive party, I would use greed, which people loved the most, to get them to give me what I wanted. I would make them their money through my marketing, advertising, and networking skills. People would always show me favour as long as I made them money.

Before birth, God had a plan for me. I had to go through these things to be able to do the task that He needed me to do. Eventually, I became great at learning every type of job to provide the service that people needed. I became a jack of all trades (sales, cutting hair, chef, landscaping, real estate, carpentry). This brings me to why I'm great at marketing, advertising, and networking. I had to learn to be good at those things to have a favour given to me.

If I wanted a nice house, then I made the developer a lot of money in order for him to allow me to live in that house. If I wanted a nice car, I had to make that car dealership a lot of money. This was learned through my experiences as a hard worker in the cotton field and a Chef in the Navy. All these things helped me become a people person and have the ability to do anything by the grace of God.

Let me ask you this question. If you owned a business and I helped you to make a million dollars, but I didn't charge you a dollar, and in return, I told you that one day I might come to you and ask you for a favour, what would you say? What would be your answer? Let's say six months pass, and I come to you and cash in on that favour and tell you I need help paying my mortgage, which is $1,500 per month.

So, you see, it's not the money I need; it's what the money could do for me. Taking it one step further, what if we applied this way of thinking to our way of life? What would be the purpose of money? We would be eliminating the source which leads to the love of money, which would be currency. This has been going on since the beginning of time. It's called the bartering system. Favour is very powerful and useful when done right. We live in a world where right is wrong and wrong is right. How much better would it be if we got back to the way things were at the beginning of time, where we would both understand and honor the bartering system?

Being able to understand this is a gift from the Lord. I was like the Chief of all sinners. I discovered that putting aside your differences for the sake of others is the true definition of love. I'm just being obedient and following in the footsteps of The Father's Son, which, at the very least, gives me the chance to give my time to those who need it, as long as it's not hindering me mentally, physically, financially, or spiritually. I'm simply along for the journey.

Understand my trials and tribulations and learn from my mistakes to better yourselves and live a more mindful life. I can't speak for everyone, but I hope we can do more for each other because we can achieve greater gifts when we work together. I only offer my opinion about the similarities between money and favour. Through my experiences, I've learned that when we are addicted to loving money, it's sinful. Actually, it's the root of all evil.

~DEEPEST THOUGHTS~

1. What **Favour** have you shown in your lifetime?

2. Who would you show **Favour** to?

3. If it's not a hindrance to your way of life, why would you be opposed to showing **Favour**?

4. Do you understand the value of **Favour** and how it can be used to supplement currency?

~CHAPTER 3~

BE FRUITFUL & MULTIPLY

Be... Before we can even get to be fruitful & multiply, we must first understand that **'B**e' has meaning as to do something. It's more of an action type of thing that comes to my mind when understanding what "**B**e" means. Looking at yourself is one of the most rewarding things you'll ever experience when you choose to "**B**e." Now, allow your mind to understand that obedience can't **be** spelled without "**B**e" being in it. I'm no teacher because there is only one Teacher, and we're just disciples of the Teacher.

I am only speaking to myself first. By God's grace, I'm trying to continue to **be** obedient to HIS WORDS and LAW." Without even realizing that you've always been obedient to something, what would it take for you to **be** honest with yourself? **B**e starts with yourself, as does everything you do because it starts with God blessing you to **be** alive.

Be, will forever **be** because of the simplicity of it. When you use the word because to someone, as you're speaking to them, you're not paying attention to that; you're about to make some excuse about something and even that can't **be** done without" **BE**." Indeed, as I was enlightened, I understood what obey meant, but if you look at the spelling, you'll also see **BE**. Being yourself starts with yourself, and recognizing the Holy Spirit on the other side of the mirror that will **be** looking back at the flesh in the world side of things.

Dive deep with me at each keyed stroke word. But, gain knowledge from them so that they have meaning to '**B**e' effective knowing that the MOST HIGH walks before you and everyone else. Before mankind, who else but THEE!

Is it not something to think about when you pay attention to all the phrases that we as beings of this world spew and believe? Even those begin with '**B**e.' First comes the A in the alphabet, but notice how "**B**" follows it, and that's when it comes back to you. Someone believing in you is a true blessing from the Most High, as it gives you another chance to be better than you were before. We can go back and forth about what '**B**e'can **be** used for, but I suggest that after reading this chapter with understanding, even then, you'll '**Be**' forever changed, all so that you can focus on what the Higher Power deems you to **be** in life.

Who are we as a race? What can we do to thrive as being in this so-called thing called life? What is it called when something is going on between a man and a woman involved? Step out of your body, look at yourself, and give yourself a real honest answer. People always ask how to do some things, and it begins with **be**. **B**e aware of your mistakes. **B**e patient with others, which will always take you to greater heights in all your ways by the grace of God.

Be a Doer of the Word instead of just speaking it aloud. **Be**friend those that God informed you to **be** with. In no way is this book going to reach everyone, but it will reach someone, which brings me back to the very first of those letters, and they believe in oneself.

Now when it comes to the religious way of doing things, my understanding is that we're to do it from a spiritual rather than the religious and human way. Nothing I'm writing down isn't in the Word of God because there's nothing new under the sun. Becoming great at something takes practice at whatever it is that you're doing. Expand your way of thinking by the grace of God, then enlightenment that you've yet to experience will **be** brought before your very spiritual being. Give thanks for some things as you and I both are very well aware that everyone has something to **be** thankful for.

I'm thankful someone believed in me enough to tell me to write a book. Life experiences will inform you if you have what it takes to gain someone's attention for that time and if they are to gain something from reading the book. What is it that the author is trying to deliver? Imagine yourself as the Chief Executive Officer of a farm that you own. What do you think it would take to deliver on time, all the time, knowing that you don't have any control over certain situations, which is the weather! What about the people in the NBA Finals, the World Series of the MLB, the Stanley Cup of the NHL or the NFL Super Bowl?

Do you believe that they all had one thing in common, and that's they all had to believe and come together as one? Take notice when you put actions behind the words you spoke of. Well, that's when mountains will **be** moved, and positive things will shape your very existence. The Most High had it written to **be** so, way before you were even born into this world of sin. Now that we've established how strong we all can **be** by the grace of God when we choose to **be**.

You see, thoughts that come to mind when I hear the word multiply are growing, gaining, progressive, benefiting, giving back, sharing, philanthropic, and selfless. To give and to give is honestly the Creator's law! Let's continue that action first. Sure, I'll take the blame for being obedient to it when others may not understand.

Only positive things will arise when we plant the seeds we desire to **be** put into our minds, body, and soul. With that understanding, it will surely **be** a harvest season of growth. How do you think you can eat the things you eat and drink the drinks you drink? It's all **be**cause, at one point, it had to **be** harvest season for that individual as well. We never seem to mind it, except when it is brought to our attention. Men lie. Women lie. Lips lie, but numbers don't. What does that have to do with what you're reading?

Even though you lack understanding right now. It doesn't mean you're incapable of gaining knowledge, wisdom, and understanding by the time you're finished. Fruitful is better viewed or seen as something prosperous or good. When the seed was sown into my understanding, it was passed down from generation to generation. That's why it states that giving is better than receiving.

I can recall many times that I needed something essential, but I had no means of obtaining it. I found myself praying to the Most-High that favour would **be** granted to me to acquire those things. It dawned on me that you reap what you sow! At that moment, I had to sow the type of seed by being fruitful in someone else's life. I had to do for others what I'd hoped to one day have someone do for me. Think of the fruits that you put into your body. Think about your reaction once you put those grapes into your mouth. Recall the moment you ate your grandmother's apple pie, your mom's sweet potato pie, and that banana pudding.

Take a stroll down memory lane and remember what that watermelon tasted like once it entered your system. All those fruits that you ate were something of greatness to your tongue. **B**eing fruitful can **be** related to being productive. Well, for me, that's what being fruitful is in life. It's the feeling of something good when you can plant great deeds in other's lives! The joy comes from within by sharing with others, knowing nothing wrong will come from doing positive things. What was sowed into my life was good fruit. There were times when a bad seed may have come into my mind, body, and soul, but in life, you must throw away the bad seeds of that fruit to get to the great one. Not all fruits will make it into the recipe, but you must choose the good ones to make them taste right and as close to perfection as possible.

What are you yielding in your way of being fruitful regarding your life and the others around you? I remember when this one time, God blessed me with a few dollars. In my mind, I already knew how I would spend the wealth given to me. Needless to say, the Most High had another thing in store for me. Little did I know that soon after, I'd meet someone who needed the exact amount God had previously granted me. It was my upbringing from the seed to **be** fruitful, and I knew then that I must

be fruitful to that individual. It wasn't my place to judge or assume that this person would hustle or manipulate me into giving my very last. All I knew is that it was my duty to **be** fruitful to that person because, just like those fruits and pies, it would **be** very constructive and of use without me knowing it, which brings me to multiply.

Just thinking about the word multiply means something is increasing. What we desire to multiply depends on what we are fruitful in planting. We can multiply our faith. We can multiply our family. We can multiply our wealth. We can multiply our status in life but make no mistake; multiplying is okay if we're planting the seeds of negativity, and even then, that's more of taking away from rather than adding to. This brings me back to what I said about Men lie. Women Lie. Lips lie, but numbers don't.

Multiply is a mathematical term. How do you think you, your children, your nieces, nephews, your mother, and your grandparents got here? They all got here by mating with one another, which then led to us multiplying in numbers. What I remember about multiplying are the times when I lied to someone; it only meant that someone lied to me ten times more than I did. So, you see, you must **be** careful about what you desire to **be** fruitful in your life because it will **be** multiplied to the highest degree.

When it was love that I desired; then I multiplied the love to someone. To **be** better at being the chef I was, I had to multiply my efforts into my craft to increase my chances of being great at what I was doing. Multiplying can **be** used for all nationalities. It's a universal language. It's used in mathematics, science, sports, entertainment, and transportation. It's even used when you desire to lengthen your hair, nails, bank account, or anything you can think of. You wouldn't say you're multiplying if you're taking from someone or some things. How could I say I am a Doer of the Word if I was stealing, scheming, or even deceiving someone and myself? All that meant was that I was subtracting, eliminating, and in no way can I say that's multiplying unless I'm removing negative things to increase the positive things.

To get the paycheck that I needed; I had to multiply my time at work, which we call overtime, to multiply my paycheck. All I had to do was look deep within myself and figure out that I needed to subtract the negative thing,

which always gave room for the more positive things. You see positives and negatives go together, which is how most things operate to move forward.
How often do you think they had to multiply the composites in your favorite shoes to make it what it is? To decrease something can lead to multiplying, but the amount of input you put into something, good or bad, will also determine how fast it will propel you. When I think of multiply, words that come to mind are, increase, reproduce, breed, procreate, and propagate. All those words are powerful when you're using them for something good. You can also multiply negative things that are going on in your life, which is what led me to get on the straight and narrow path. Other words associated with multiply would grow, accumulate, proliferate, and mount up.

As I looked into the mirror, I found the better side of who I was destined to **be**. I realized then that to multiply whatever good was inside meant that I couldn't associate myself with words such as decrease and diminish if I genuinely needed the Most-High to extend my life. To follow in Yahweh's footsteps also meant that I had to double down on my goal. I had to enlarge my faith if I was to **be** able to move forward. In what areas are you expanding your life to multiply the things that are of need rather than your wants? What would it take to build you up to the point of no return so you could achieve the maximum amount of will within?

Life will only **be** extended to you, as it's been done for me. But only you can honestly say that you chose to **BE** FRUITFUL & MULTIPLY about all the positive things that are in all of us. We must all multiply those efforts and spread the love, wealth, knowledge, wisdom, and pain that we went through helping others reach their potential. I so desire to rise as a human race.

Who am I? I am who I am, and I pray that the Almighty will double down on my way of **Be**ing so that I may **BE** FRUITFUL & MULTIPLY all the good in me so that all the blessings granted to me may **be** passed on to you.

I never desire to compress what's been shared to get me to this place. This book of understanding will help you not destroy, but rather employ you to greater heights in all your ways, just as it's done mine. Don't decline your faith, but rather allow it to incline you to **be** better than yesterday because I can assure you that to multiply isn't to reduce or divide you in no way, shape, or form.

Did you hit the pay dirt in any areas of your way of thinking? What gave you the strength to push ahead when there were doubtful moments in your life? We must continue to make headway in all of our ways of doing things if we're to weather the storms of adversity. It will only **be** in our best interest if we hide or conceal things when we try our best to become the superior version of ourselves. While reading this, you'll do so with the understanding that some of those words aren't in any way positive. Are you ready to **BE** FRUITFUL and MULTIPLY?

~NOTES~

~DEEPEST THOUGHTS~

1. What fruits are you planting in your mind, body and soul?

2. Are you multiplying negative things in your thinking and heart?

3. When do you choose to be something?

4. What would you desire to be after looking yourself in the mirror?

~Chapter 4~

THE WORLD IS A HYPOCRITE

I shall only start this chapter off by including myself first. We often do things without realizing that we're doing them until it's already done. Can you say we can handle the truth when it's brought to us? Are you willing to accept what the truth is? Can you put yourself in those same shoes and not wither or run from what is? What is your character made of? Who is the blame for the chaos that's being brought upon you?

Before I dive deeper into this chapter, let's first establish what a hypocrite truly is. This will be someone who delves into hypocrisy. It's the action of someone saying they believe in something or someone, but their actions are the opposite. It's like saying that I have faith but then questioning someone or something with a doubtful mindset or action. Being deceitful to yourself would be the same as being a hypocrite.

Back in the Navy, I can recall having to do all the work because let's face it, I was the newbie. I was just an E-3 in rank, so everyone above outranked me. I still remember them having to do everything because I was fresh on the ship. I can't say that they haven't done them because, as a chef in the Navy, we all had to do it at some point in our careers. It's those moments when you've graduated from those positions, and then they'll hit you with one of these numbers. "Hey, Razorback.....will you mind doing my meal prep?"

As a youngster, I had no idea that they were playing me. I'm all happy to go lucky with believing that they had a genuine love for me. So I did the work. "No problem. I'll do it. Just don't forget when it's my time to ask you to do something for me." "No problem Razorback." We always used last names or places where we were from to communicate with one another.

Well, the time had passed, and we may have been on the way to Israel, and I had that particular weekend off, and I was happy as all outdoors to be this young pupil about to explore what being overseas was all about. Well, one day before we even made it over there, I asked the same person who had asked me for a favour, if they would do the same for me. Well, I'm hoping that you'll knock out my last portion of my duties, so I can catch up with everyone and have everyone show me around the cities." She was like, "well Razorback, you know I have a lot to do and I just don't have the time to do it for you." So, I went to her, and I was like, "hey, you remember when you asked me to do your work that one time?" my response to her was. "But you said you'd help me when I came to you, and now that I'm here asking for the same thing that you asked me for. Now you want to give all types of excuses and explain why you won't. Cool, one day you'll be asking me to do something else, and then I'll remind you how you were such a hypocrite."

Throughout my lifetime, there have been many situations in which I remember how hypocrisy has been such a negative in my life because it's always been when I needed it the most that I was denied the same thing that I had given, only for it to come back and not be received. As I sit here reflecting on many other occasions, I'm like, hey, I'm going to do this, I'm going to do that, but unless they see it, they don't believe it.

Let's role reverse and imagine someone telling you the same thing. They would like for you to believe in what they're saying and doing without proof. They want you to believe in them but choose not to believe you. I can't speak for others, but I'd like to voice my opinion, and that's someone that you can call a hypocrite. Are there any scenarios where you've been on the giving end to someone expecting it to be reciprocated in the same manner, only for it not to happen? Well, that's what you would call a hypocrite.

What I'm speaking about isn't something that hasn't been done in this world. It's just that we lack the understanding of how often it's being done to us or how often we do it ourselves. I'm not the most brilliant tack in the toolbox, but even I can understand hypocrisy in its most valid form.

Have you ever experienced situations where people you've voted for claimed they would provide better roads? They expressed how they would give better healthcare, only for you to experience a total letdown once they're in the office. I never speak of something or someone without doing it myself first because that's where everything starts, which is why the Holy Spirit is within. Can I look myself in the mirror and ask the question myself as if I've ever been a pretender, and the answer to that would be yes? Anyone with understanding would know that to pretend is to be a hypocrite if my recollection serves me right. I do believe that I may have back-slided a few times throughout my life.

Now please understand this book is my point of view, hoping that with it, I'll get better at all those things written about. Are you part of the world? Do you reside on this planet? Do you make up a population of a certain race? I'm not pointing the finger; I'm only asking the questions to myself and anyone reading this book. If your answer to those questions is yes, then you're part of the world.

There's no escaping what can't be escaped. What is a bigot? Isn't it the same as being a hypocrite? Is it my fault if you happen to fall into that category? Once again, that's what we call a hypocrite. Am I the blame for something you are once you understand that some of what you're reading applies to you? What harm can come from putting in the effort, to be honest in what you say and do? Is it such a bad thing to be truthful with ourselves so we can be truthful to everyone else? Can you say you're being a hypocrite because you're straightforward? I'd have to be in denial if I was to tell you I was upstanding 24/7 of the year. If I admit to that, I'd be doing the very thing I'm writing about.

Surrounding yourself with dependable people will only lead you to become more dependable. Are we able to accept the bad with the good, with the understanding of what being a hypocrite means? When pen meets paper, I'm thinking about a moment when the opportunity to do double-dealing was there for the taking. I can't explain to you why I chose not to be rebellious. Who am I to even try and judge myself because it clearly states, in the religious sense, that only God can judge you?

Is it too much to ask for a candid conversation so our actions may be candid? It's funny to see our ways when we're being honest with ourselves. If I had a dollar for every time, I heard someone call me a fraud, I'd have more currency than Jeff Bezos. They do not even realize that, at the very instance, they're being hypocrites. What sense does it make to practice bad faith? How does that benefit you, me, and us as a whole? Indeed, that's something to think about. It wouldn't be too far-fetched to associate that lip service with being a hypocrite. Calculating the times that people have told me to give up and that I would never succeed. Can't you take one piece of the bible and not take the other? You can't speak it into existence unless you speak it. It repeatedly tells you to have faith.

How often are we paying attention to what's being learned? Those things I've said to others may not have happened when I said them, but that doesn't mean they didn't happen. It just meant those individuals weren't there to witness it, but the world can be a hypocrite sometimes without even knowing it.

Are there areas in your life where there were double standards? Well, could you also say that's hypocritical? Have I been looked at as a sham? Of course, I have, but that also goes back to what is being written about the world as a hypocrite. It was by choice on my behalf to learn how to be forthright. I'd be lying if I can say the change came overnight too. Not realizing how much I overreached is how I learned I was a hypocrite.

Understanding it was God's grace!

Have you found yourself in situations where you knew the Holy Spirit was speaking to you, but for some reason, you may have ignored it and done the opposite or nothing at all? Well, allow me to educate you. That's the same as being a hypocrite. Speaking from a spiritual point of view. I may not be quoting it word for word, but my understanding of what's done in the dark will come to light. Well, this will also fall under the hypocrisy of life.

How can I truly say I'm following in the footsteps of Yahweh, but my actions weren't the same? To hit the summit of my thinking meant that I had to do away with old patterns of such. It meant that my words had to follow my thinking, and actions soon followed my words. Can anyone reading this book relate to ever experiencing situations where things were said, could be done, only not for it to take place? A boxed mentality only meant you'd be limited in your thinking capacity.

You'd have to be an out-of-the-box thinker to most likely understand the point of view that I'm speaking of, and even then, its simplicity is what needs to be understood. Most of the time, we choose not to look at ourselves in the mirror, for we know that we'd be looking at the hypocrite at the precise moment.

There's no need to be upset for falling into the same category as someone who tends to be late all the time but throws a hissy fit the moment someone shows up late! I hate to say it, but the truth is told, that's also why we are all hypocrites. It wasn't long after I saw that light that I decided not to say, LORD. I made up my mind that my actions would follow just as well.

It was then that I needed to allow the light to reflect my choice to be obedient. It wasn't something I had to say anymore because I didn't have to worry about being a hypocrite by doing things this way. I was no longer speaking about what I was going to do or speaking about the Lord. I was being about my actions, as well as being about the Lord's business too.

God knows all of our hearts, so what we speak is something that He already knows. It's the stuff within your hearts which matters most to the Almighty! I didn't start giving to charity to go out there and announce to the world. I may not know the scriptures from the bible verbatim, but I do understand the understanding taught to me by someone who had the simplest ways to break things down.

Words that can be associated with being a hypocrite would be these of such. Proud comes to mind. Boastful is another, but most people don't pay attention because of being truthful. These are the negatives that are aligned with being a hypocrite. Let's not act like there haven't been scary moments in our lives; even that is part of the hypocrisy. I can only speak about the facts of life as I've experienced them, and in no way is my understanding the end of all.

I'm only relating to things that will give you pause and something to think about. What's the real reason we say we're compassionate to someone else? Are we doing it for the right reasons, or are we doing it for the benefits that can come from it? Even then, we can say it's hypocritical. To be secure isn't for you to be insecure because without you realizing it, you're being a hypocrite.

Are you someone who needs to be praised by others? We never really pay attention to our actions until it's brought to the forefront. Now don't go beating yourself up about it. Just make the change if that's important to you.

Are you one of those people who tends to offer your advice, but when it comes to taking heed to the advice you're giving, you tend to shy away from it? Well, that's someone who'll be classified as a hypocrite too. What would you call me if I was to masquerade around portraying, I was the best at what I could do but when it came down to delivering, all I had for you was excuses and more deadlines? Allow me to answer it for you so I don't put you in a place of being judgmental. It's called being a hypocrite.

This chapter isn't some decoy wrapped up to make you feel good in no way. This chapter is to have you pay more attention to how far gone we are into the world rather than the WORD! This chapter is designed to hurt as if salt is poured into an open womb. It's supposed to cause you to think about what was, what is, and what will be. I always wondered why I never went down the road of acting. As I got older, I understood why it wasn't for me.

Being an actor means you have to portray yourself as something you're not. You're acting as an impostor. Don't get me wrong, but isn't that just the same as being a hypocrite?

Being a hypocrite can change you for the better when you truly allow the Holy Spirit to transform you. So, before you point the finger, please remember that these are my points of view. I'm merely an instrument to help you understand the true meaning of things, and that's by the grace of God.

What are the positives that come from being a hypocrite? In what areas would you be positioning your family by being hypocritical? Being able to be truthful and letting actions come into play, of course, with practice and patience, we would have, without a shadow of a doubt, stared hypocrisy in its face and let our light shine. Many times, over, I've had people tell me that they were genuine, but their actions represented that of a backstabber. I soon learned that anything in my life happened for a reason. It's up to us and us to understand the reasoning. Maybe being late a few minutes might be hypocritical because you don't like it being done to you. What if being late led to you being in the right place at the right time? It could also cause you not to get caught up in that traffic jam because you decided to leave late. Now, in no way am I justifying being a hypocrite.

I'm just pointing out the cause behind the effect. With that being said, I'm hoping it will also get you to practice better habits by doing things with added time. We always ask for things to be better or pray to a Higher Power, but we never really pay attention to the source itself, and that's us as the human race.

We're so busy being hypocrites that we're missing the best thing about it all, and that is it starts with us, so we have the chance to change the hypocrisy. How would you view me if I was standing behind the pool pit and I gave a sermon about infidelity and how it tells us in the Word of God how we're to be faithful in all of our ways? Then on a particular night, you see me with another woman other than my wife. Would you be judgmental? Would you point the finger at my flaws? Although you and I both know it's hypocritical.

When we take matters into our own hands by playing God, we become hypocrites. What right do I have to gossip about anyone or anything when I don't want those things happening to me? What examples am I displaying by telling someone to do something I wouldn't do? Being simple in life won't confuse you. It won't cause disturbance in your life either. This is why when you look at the hypocrisy of life, it's all too simple to ask the question, are you a hypocrite? Blessed are those who can choose to look in the mirror and acknowledge who they are, good or bad! I will applaud anyone willing to put aside their differences by being honest with themselves. Because that is the only way we can end the hypocrisy of the world is when we start with ourselves.

~DEEPEST THOUGHTS~

1. What in this chapter can you relate to about hypocrisy?

2. Have you ever been a hypocrite?

3. After reading this chapter, what are the bullet points that resonated with you the most?

4. Why do you think us as a human race deal with hypocrisy when it's nothing good?

~Chapter 5~

Putting Aside Your Differences

She was pregnant in 1974 at the age of 15. A child in herself, who knew what would be born in the 70s to a 16-year-old teenager from the South? At this moment, the meaning of putting aside your differences was displayed at that very instance of understanding that you are with a child! A Mother's Love!

Born with a veil over the body of this spiritual being was only the beginning of what God blessed to be born into this world of sin. A decision could have been made to abort me, or I could have been put up for adoption. But NO!

The young mother-to-be chose to bring this child into the world. Small in stature was this young lady herself. Born was the King that God placed into the heart of this young infant; the responsibility was placed upon me without even knowing it. Being your Great-Grandmother's oldest Great-Grandson. Your Grandmother's oldest Grandson and your Mother's oldest son.

I can still remember everything from the age of 3 years old. Even at that young age, I knew I was different. Taught to love wholeheartedly without a shadow of a doubt was beaten into me at a very young age.
Turning the other cheek would be the same as putting aside your differences.

Parents need to pay more attention to how much their children are being observant to their every saying and doing. No woman should ever have to go through what my Mother went through. Was it love that she was demonstrating, or was it putting aside her differences for the sake of her children's father? The book of the Bible was what my Granny taught me. It was always the same thing, "Saul did this baby, and Saul did that." I never entirely understood why she kept calling me Saul, but it will all make sense to you as we near the end of this book. Out by the radio station was this tiny little house with an outhouse with fields of cotton and wheat surrounding it. This home had no carpet, just a tin box with plumbing and dirt for the hardwood floor, which had to be constantly swept until it was smooth like marble due to the dust.

Our bathtub was made of metal; we had to manually turn and pull our clothes through our metal washing machine by hand. You want to talk about growing up poor as if it was still slavery.

God allowed me to see the tail end of it, and I can tell you that the love was confirmed in our household. My Grandmother was the oldest of 12 kids. She had nine kids, 49 grandchildren, 82 great-grandchildren, and 13 great, great-grandchildren.

We grew up as the type of family where love flowed abundantly. Everyone had to put aside their differences because the home was at least 750 square feet. Due to the small living quarters, there wasn't any room for "E.G.O," which means (Easing. God. Out.), to be upset. In those days, growing up the way I did, everything was shared. It had its pros and cons in such a large family. But the values of what family means came from the root of God passed down to this being of the man I am today. Patience comes to mind when you associate the word love with anything. It's one of those words that means the exclusion of our wants and needs for the sake of others. It covers a multitude of sins as long as it's done in the correct practice of the Word of God. It can hurt when you have to tell the truth, but telling a lie would be more hurtful. Being in a relationship means you have to put aside your differences. You would disapprove of your spouse cheating on you, so don't cheat on them. That deep affection you have for something, or someone was something I had to sacrifice to honestly say I understood what being obedient to the law meant.

To say that I love God meant that I had to put aside my mischievous ways to say I was undoubtedly following in the footsteps of Yahweh! I had to do away with those lying habits if I was to say that I understood something. I was no longer obsessed with worldly things which had no value. Would I give those things I had plenty of to someone in need?

You see, I can only drive one car at a time. With that being said, why did I need so many? What type of person with multiple vehicles denies someone who didn't have transportation or needed a ride, knowing that it could benefit someone other than yourself would be the most honorable thing to have done.

It's showing love to that person, according to the Bible.

God put aside His differences and gave His only begotten Son to pay a debt He didn't owe all because we owed a debt that we couldn't pay. Are we better than God that we can't put aside our differences for the sake of something or someone to ensure that LOVE will never fail, as long as we're obedient? Hmmm...

Still wet behind the ears, as they would say below the Mason Dixon line when speaking about the inexperience one might need to improve. Most of the time, you'd have to be at the family reunion to gain all this knowledge from the old souls.

If I'm not mistaken, there are about 600+ still alive in my family. Some are straight. Some are gay. Some are tall, and some are small. A few may be unhappy with their weight, but that's for them. Some went to college; others chose not to. There might have been a few who sold drugs and some who indulged in them. No matter what, we all had to put aside our differences for the sake of our family. There's a difference between being someone's relative and being their family.

As I sit here and recall being in Kentucky, the sacrifices that had to be made from all the generations of birth from our ancestors left us with many lessons that had to be learned. I was there visiting, and my aunt and uncle as they slept in bed.

My cousin and I, who are no longer with us, decided to sneak outside while everyone was asleep. Well, all I remember was telling him not to drop me. In case you're wondering, I was hanging from the sheet from a five-story building my cousin had me dangling from. He assured me he wouldn't drop me, but I kept hearing him say, I'm slipping. Soon after, my aunt and uncle came barging in to save me from being killed from the drop to the ground. I wouldn't be here today had they not come in when they did. When it came down to taking the blame, neither of us would point the finger at the other. We put aside our differences to take the blame so the other wouldn't get into trouble. Now that's what you call love at its finest!

Now, let's go back to a young girl raising a child. My Mother was a 9th-grade dropout. She put aside her differences to ensure I was fed, clothed, and cared for to the best of her ability. We were beginning to integrate races when racism was at its highest. You can only imagine what a young mother with a child during a racist era had to endure.

Having to swallow her pride from being called all types of names. I know all too well about having to put aside my differences growing up with the family I had.

Constantly being bullied, I guess you say I learned how to accept being pushed over, beaten on, and down to verbal abuse because all I ever knew was to put aside my differences for the sake of others. After all, that's what I saw my Mother doing.

Having to dumb myself down just to fit in was one of the ways I learned to cut the bullying down. Not being in the spotlight meant fewer people would recognize me. Making sure that I pleased others was all that I understood. Although the pain I felt was nerve-wracking, it was no comparison to what the Creator's Son had to endure. Coming home with many black eyes, busted lips, and anything you would think of, it had to happen to me, but remember, all I understood was to put aside my differences for the sake of others. Of course, it had its ups and downs, now that I reflect on it. It built a sense of character in me. It taught me how to stand firm. The irony is that the guy who bullied me the most, later on down the line, would play a pivotal part in my growth in life. All my life, I was brainwashed into thinking I had to take the blame for things and put aside my differences to get people to like me.

Traveling to Texas in the Chevy Tahoe, my tire had a blowout. I had no credit card, cash, or anything. All I had was that check in my briefcase. So, I was forced to cash the check.

I gave the young man the money and proceeded with our journey.

Well, we ended up doing business and went out that night. I'm not paying attention to the date. The next day, it's Friday the 13th, and we're traveling back home on Highway 59 north. I remember looking at the State Trooper as he was traveling southbound. Next thing I know, he's turning around and has his lights and siren on. He pulls up and asks for the license and registration. I'm nervous because I know that there are five pounds of marijuana behind me, not hiding or anything. I mean in plain sight.

So, I pulled over and put the truck in park. We were just about done with him, and he was about to leave, and that's when this other trooper pulled up and asked, what was that? I didn't reply, nor did the guy I was trying to please. Then they pulled it out and put it on the trooper's car. They walked back over and asked me the question again. Who does it belong to?

I said, "it's not mine, sir." He looked at my so-called friend and asked him the same question. Who does this belong to? In my head, I'm thinking I know he's going to take ownership of his turf.

You have to understand where I'm from. You open your mouth and snitch, you die. Then he replied and said, "it's not mine either, sir." The officer looked at me and said that since neither of you want to take ownership of it, we're charging the owner of this vehicle with possession of marijuana with the intent to distribute. I'm telling myself that this can't be happening to me.

My Grandmother was right. She told me not to cash that check because something terrible would happen.

Fast forward a few years, and now I'm in prison. I was supposed to be in a minimum-security type of place, but God had other plans for me because they left me in a

maximum security prison amongst killers, rapists, crime bosses, and gang leaders.
The first law of nature is self-preservation. I'll never forget when I went to my cell the guard said you might as well drop your bags and everything. Next thing you know, a white guy, a black fellow, backed by a Hispanic and Asian, was beating and stomping on me. All I knew was what was instilled in me, and that was to defend myself.

Being beaten to a pulp, I heard the tank boss say that's enough; he's worthy enough as a man. The next thing you know, they were helping me up and helping me to my bunk, which was the top bunk. It reminded me of the movie 'Life' regarding the setup of the prison. Forty-eight inmates were in a metal house with no phones to contact family or anything. It seemed like a dream until one day, the dream never ended.

It may have been about the 1st week there, and I remembered they had some bible study.
For some odd reason, I have no idea why I chose to say something. I asked them if I could join them. They said sure you can. You have to lead, though, and as I

remembered my teaching from my Grandmother. Psalms 91 was one of my favorites, so I taught about a time of trouble on that particular subject. What I didn't know was that I was good at it.

The next night, they asked if I would be attending bible study. I told them not tonight; I'm going to sleep. Let me tell you something, boy, was I in for a rude awakening?

I mean, all those guys gathered around my bunk and said, Hey look, I don't know who taught you how to break down that bible like that, but if you don't come back and break down that bible to us for the duration of your stay here, then you're not going to make it out of here alive.

Well, at that instance, I decided to pick up the bible and start with the enlightenment of educating those other inmates about the laws of the Bible and the Quran. Did I want to give up what freedom I did have to do that every night? The answer to that would be no.

I hated having to sacrifice my time.

A year has now passed, and I have another year to go. I'm getting comfortable now. I've seen things inside those walls that you only see in movies. Then more time passed, and I was getting ready to get out. The same way you came into the prison is the same way you had to leave.

I'll never forget being on the bus with 26 guys on death row. That meant they were never going to get out. The memories of when they all approached me and said, hey Minnesota, do you know the only reason you're getting out of here? I said because it's my time to do so. They said no, it's because you kept your mouth shut. It's because you chose not to be a rat.

We know everything about you. We know it wasn't your drugs. We know you served in the military. We know you're more of a nerd. Allow us to tell you this, stop hanging around the people who don't mean you any good. Give up trying to please people who don't care about anything but themselves. The guards don't run these prisons, the inmates run them. We run them from all over the world. The next time you're in jail, we'll kite you and have you killed! You're one of the good ones.

If the question arises as to how is that beneficial? Well, it all stems back to what I witnessed as a child. I've seen my mom keep her mouth closed when she was beaten physically and verbally. I would always keep my mouth closed as I was bullied as a child and throughout adulthood, and to have kept my mouth closed, which was the only reason I got a pass.

Although I ended up in a hostile place, I witnessed negative things. It's putting aside your differences and showing love. It's the reason God spared my life. Through the journey and experience of being incarcerated, I learned to be a speaker and a doer of the word. There will always be moments when you can choose to be selfish, or you can choose to do what God has done for all of humanity, and that's putting aside our differences for the sake of others by showing love because surely you'd desire for someone to show you the same compassion if there was ever a time you needed it the most.

Are you willing to do it for the right reasons in life? Good things happen to bad people, and bad things happen to good people, but who are we to play God and judge when we don't want to be judged? So, put aside your differences and show love, for it will cover a multitude of sins.

~DEEPEST THOUGHTS~

1. What does putting aside your differences mean to You?

2. How can we put aside our differences as a human race to benefit us as a whole?

3. Who would you put aside your differences for and why?

4. Can you see the similarities between putting aside your own differences and love?

~Chapter 6~

'HONESTY'

HELPING. OVERCOME. NEGATIVITY. EVERYDAY. STARTS THROUGH YOU

Where does it begin? Does it start with others, or does it start from within?

The Holy Spirit resides in us all, so it must go through us to rub off on everyone surrounding us.

It's what defines us as spiritual beings. So where does being dishonest hail from?

What triggers one to be dishonest? I'm merely offering my opinion, but greed comes to mind when I think of being a liar.

As my memories serve me, I'm referencing when my Mom asked me where I'd been. Realizing now that my answers weren't always the truth, I can understand the root of things now. How could I ever gain God's grace when my actions were disgraceful? It wasn't far finding the answers to the questions I was seeking as I constantly asked God for His mercy and grace. It was revealed that the Holy Spirit from within possesses it.

Is there truth about the honesty which was written in the Good Book? Principles are there for a reason. It's the alignment that keeps us balanced in life by the grace of God. Where's the deceit in straightforwardness?

We should always have some self-respect about ourselves. The genuine inside of you should be coming off and be as radiant as the solar flares coming from the sun. One must be put into the position to know what it feels like to be betrayed, to understand how important it is to be loyal.

The Most High knows all of our inner secrets and thoughts. It's impossible to hide from the Creator of life. Even the most straightforward questions that deserve simple answers aren't the truth.

An example of what I'm saying is when my Granny and Captain ask me what I did the night before. If my answer isn't true, I only need to look at myself for being dishonest. Would it have bothered me if someone had been dishonest with me? What type of fruit did I possess in my mind, body, and soul?

Was it the fruitfulness of deceit?

Were they fruits of entrusting, evil, fraudulence, and treachery?

The moment of truth, as I stared into the mirror, looking the Holy Spirit in the eyes. The words came out of my mouth as smooth as water, and all I said was stop using God's name in vain if your corrupt actions will stay the same. Am I speaking the truth when I say that lying lips aren't being faithful to the Holy Spirit? If I'm not mistaken, the

Holy Spirit resides within you. So, if you're lying to the Holy Spirit, you're lying to yourself. So, in what way can you say that's honesty?

To break the bondage cycle, I knew that I had to speak the truth in the checkout line at about 8:00 am on this cold morning in the twin cities. Standing in the checkout line, I know it's going to be about $300 in groceries. Bagging everything up, I reach into my pocket and pull out the money and passed it to the cashier lady. She gives me back my change and I'm knowing how much I should be getting back. As I was leaving, I noticed she had given me too much. I handed the lady the change she gave me and told her she had miscounted although it was only .50 cents.

You have to pay attention to what really matters.

How can the Holy Father trust you to handle a large amount of wealth when you can't even do right with the smallest?

We always tend to want to call on God when we need something, but we never choose to do right by God in the slightest ways.

That way is starting by being honest with yourself.

Everything in life is visible to the Holy Spirit. We, as a human race, can do nothing to change it. We can only change the spirit from within.

All my life, I felt I was put here for a greater purpose. I'm laughing as I write this chapter because of all those negative things I've done from lying, cheating, deceiving, manipulating, and being downright a menace. I now understand that I needed to get to this point. It was a life lesson that I was to learn from.

The two most important days of your life would be the day you're born, and the day you understand your purpose and why you're even here in the 1st place.

There's nothing sexy about a King or Queen being called a liar. It's a lot easier to tell the truth. Truth saves a ton of time. It eliminates you having to keep up the lie in the first place. I know all too well how lying can lead to other things.

I sincerely hope that by taking the time to obtain the information you're reading; you allow the spirit from within to lead you all your way.

To have fidelity is to have trust. To have infidelity is when there's no trust. My bluntness isn't the best as it relates to how I communicate, but the one thing you can say is that I AM being honest with myself.

I'm preparing myself for the aftermath soon after this book is published, but nobody will be able to say that I'm being dishonest. The choice will be ours. This book reflects on oneself and how to move forward in life. I'm no longer interested in how things can be done by taking shortcuts. I'm not giving in to corruption because things are moving slower than I would like.

When we choose to be deceitful, we're putting others at a disadvantage, and for that reason. I choose to show mercy with my speech because I hope to have the same in return. Being dishonest will either be a handicap, a hindrance, or both.

I had to learn to do away with the evil way of thinking for others to be truthful to me.

Allow me to explain why I'm not better than Jesus or Yahweh. I hate my flesh. The flesh might start you off smiling, but before the days are over, it will always end in a frown.

It's fragile, and it will decay, and that's why we should pray. Not one day, but every day. I know about flesh; it's a sinful thing. I also know about God and His mighty hand. God's hand is so powerful that he can pull you in and place His love deep within. The flesh can steal, and it will kill, but God can heal if we would just be still.

So, excuse me, Heavenly Father, for I know I have sinned. I don't know where to start or begin, but I do know my life on the day may end. This life will have you on a journey that you can't withstand, but by His will only, and that takes place when we all comprehend.

So, in the beginning, let me start by saying AMEN. Forgive me, Father, for I know not what I do, but when I learn better, allow me to do better, and that's for the Glory of YOU.

So, it's time to right the wrong, and that's merely for the strong. "Children go where I send thee; how shall I send thee." I love the lyrics to that song. I only pray I can be about my Father's business of demonstrating.

H.O.N.E.S.T.Y.

~DEEPEST THOUGHTS~

1. Can you say you've been completely honest with yourself?

2. What about this chapter would you say at some point you were at those crossroads?

3. When would you say is the right to time to be honest?

4. What is your understanding of honesty?

~Chapter 7~

'WISDOM'

(WEALTHY INSIGHTFULNESS SPREAD DOWN ONTO MINDS)

Wisdom is a magical word when we apply it to our daily actions. Wisdom is quality when you pay attention to it, truth be told. I'll always look at that myself and speak to it before I do it to others. When decisions are made and the outcome is negative, you understand it before you make a choice. Then can you say that you used wisdom in the process? I've learned throughout my lifespan that you'll always use sound wisdom in your choice-making when and if you do this before making any decisions.

I've asked myself if I can live with the outcome of my fate because of my good or bad choices. I then said that if I could, then make a choice. You'd be amazed at how often I soon started making wise decisions.

Where would I be in life had I made better choices in my early years?

Indeed, others ask themselves what it would be like if we could go back in time.

When you start making wise choices, you'll find yourself in a better space where you won't have to ask those questions because you would've used sound wisdom. Can you say you've used wisdom if you chose to drink and drive and damaged your vehicle or killed someone? As spiritual beings, we must always strive to obtain wisdom in every way possible. My definition of wisdom would be **"WEALTHY INSIGHTFULNESS SPREAD DOWN ONTO MINDS."** I'll be the first person to tell you that I only sometimes used sound wisdom.

All my teachings and values were lost once I left the nest at home. It wasn't anyone there to be in your ear every day. There wasn't the much-needed guidance to navigate you through that thing we call life. All I had was wisdom passed down from generation to generation that was instilled in me by my grandmother, my mother, and any other elder. Wisdom has been here since the beginning of time. Having wisdom and understanding is what separates you from others who are struggling.

In no way can you say wisdom has ever harmed anyone. Can we look at ourselves and say we've never used wisdom? The world doesn't owe us anything but death because life isn't promised. I thank God for the poise I learned while in the military.

At the time, I thought I was being punished. Little did I know that this was all in God's plan for me. Only sometimes do we understand why good things happen to bad people and bad things happen to good people, and I can appreciate the wisdom I gained from enduring life experiences.

Here it comes. You're under arrest for possession of marijuana. Embarrassing, to say the least. I'm now a Navy Veteran with a felony on his record. In my mind, I think that my life is over. The best advice I can give any child is to be more patient about growing up because of your inability to use wisdom. Trust me when I tell you that when it rains, it pours.

Now you have to deal with the court systems; you have to deal with the lawyers, financing, and traveling. All this is because of the choice of not using sound wisdom. No matter what, there are two sides to everything and everyone. Are we born with wisdom? Is a newborn child born with wisdom? At what point do we, as a race, decide to apply the wisdom that we've learned to our daily routine? Forgive me, as I must stay on track. It's imperative that I remain focused, which leads me to the following scenario.

There are up to 30 years of living that's taking place up to this point, not to mention having a little bit of money, so you think you're the I.T.! Low and behold, the reality starts sinking in, and you realize that this is the norm on a daily and consistent basis.

I hope the understanding God has given me to enlighten everyone reading this book will benefit you all. I'm using the wisdom of pointing out all of my flaws to eliminate or give others the power to manipulate and deceive you. The wisdom is to be passed on to the ones you leave behind. It's not yours to be selfish because your life doesn't belong to you.

Consider Dion Sanders, who's played in the super bowl, the World Series, and other things. Does he have much to offer the younger generations that came after him? Doing it at the level that he's done has required him to know how to use wisdom. The wisdom helped him to be the best shutdown corner to have ever lived, but at the end of the day, it's only my opinion that's being offered. Allow me to give you something else to think about regarding wisdom. Even Michael Jordan wouldn't be who he is today had it not been for the best player he's ever known, and that's his brother. It's the wisdom that he had passed down to him that granted him the opportunity to be the G.O.A.T. to have played the game of basketball, and even that is someone's opinion.

The insight from business owners to the wealthy people of the earth can also be credited to the wisdom that got them to where they are now. The sapiens of any one of your grandparents is how you can live the life you have. I still grasp what I learned from others of my past, no matter who they may have come from, because there's always room for improvement in our daily lives.

It may not be me that you will take heed from, but even the intellect that you gain from scholars in school can also be called wisdom.

Wisdom doesn't come overnight. It comes with time, and this brings me to the next chapter.

Who is to say we have it to obtain because time isn't promised to anyone but itself? What wisdom can you apply to yourself to move forward in the best way for you? What wisdom will you pass down to your children so they can pass it down to their own?

What wisdom will you choose to pull you out of the situation you may be in that's hindering you? Would you choose wisdom over anything that's negative which can set you back? Would you consider the wisdom you're gaining from paying attention to this book as something positive? What would you call the astuteness of Oprah Winfrey, Steve Jobs, Warren Buffett, Elon Musk, and Jeff Bezos? Can we agree that they, too, may have gained the wisdom to put them at the top of the world's wealthiest elites? Well, that's what **W.I.S.D.O.M.** is.

Its **WEALTHY INSIGHTFULNESS SPREAD DOWN ONTO MINDS**. I challenge you to download those six words into your brain to catapult you into that same level, and I can assure you that you, too, will be at the top just as they are.

~NOTES~

~DEEPEST THOUGHTS~

1. What does wisdom mean to you?

2. What did you get from reading this chapter?

3. Would you apply wisdom in all your ways of living?

4. When should wisdom be applied in life?

~Chapter 8~

TIME "TRANSITIONING. INTO. MOMENTS. ETERNITY."

I can tell you this for starters. It's the one thing that's everlasting. It will always be here for the age to come. There's no existence without it. Whether you're discussing yesterday, today, a season, or the future, you'll constantly be referencing time.

How much of it do you have? Nobody in this world can say they know the beginning and the end. What we can do is hope for another day. Praying that we will be granted another moment to do whatever we need the time for.

When you talked about a specific game for which your favorite team and player played. You're still speaking about time. It's the one thing that's priceless. You can't buy time.

Time doesn't owe me or anyone in this world its privilege. I'm sure, as most will be reading this chapter at some point, you'll look at your clock; rather it's in your car, on your wrist, or in your house. There's no escaping time.

How is your time broken up to maximize the allotment of it that God has blessed you with? Do you have it to give? For the ones who are parents. What would you give to have that extra time with your precious babies? How about this for an example? It's been about 5-plus years since my Granny left the flesh and placed into the dirt, as I know her spirit remains.

As a child, I never envisioned that my Granny would someday not be here to touch. The lack of understanding has yet to reach its full potential up to this point. I do remember those naps before I got disciplined. I also recall when she would have me typing out church programs before I knew how to type. The reflections stored in my memory are those moments in time. What about the fans at a football game during the super bowl, and the game is a tie with a certain number of seconds left on the clock? The reference of time will occur throughout the day. It lives with us for eternity. You can only mention when your child is born by mentioning time in the same fashion. How often is the time taken for granted? Now back to my Granny. She once told me I didn't do much for her when she was alive, but I'd do

much for her when she was gone. I didn't understand it at the time, but I'm looking at it now. I understand even when you mention the word generation. You're speaking of time. Even using the word in this sentence, "this very instant is a time reference. Have you ever heard the saying, “you do the crime, you do time?”
Well, that's exactly what I had to do when I joined the military. I had to do my time in service.

Do you know the similarities between military service and prison? When you're in both, they require you to do your time. What comes to mind when you hear the words fall, spring, summer, and winter? I'll tell you what comes to mind when I hear those words. It's time in itself. Is it not? I understood my Granny when she told me I'd do more for her when she's gone. Have you ever seen a relationship where she or you tell one another that you both should take a break? Is that too also something to think about? At what stage of your life did it all start to click for you? If we're ever to change these generational curses, then we must prepare for the day when we're no longer here to be able to be that provider and protector.

Time is the one thing that will be here for eternity. It's also a very longshot for a rich man to make it into the gates of heaven than for a camel to fit through the eye of a needle. Allow me to demonstrate how focusing on the past can happen.

Imagine yourself traveling down a street. Now you're faced with the opposition of navigating through complex challenges. One false move can be fatal for you and anyone you fail to run into. Depending upon the collision's severity, it could also end somebody's life. The moral to all these words flowing through me is consistently words that are synonyms for time. When you think you know it all, will be the moment that time informs you who's first. The only being that can defeat time is the Creator of time. If you didn't know, reading this chapter will enlighten you. You'll always try to catch up to time, but it'll never happen, but rest assured that time will always catch up to you... Even as I write this chapter, I have to deal with time because of the deadline my publisher gave me to finish the book so it can go to editing, etc. At this precise moment, I put the pen down to grab a bite to eat, and right there in front of me on the television was a certain program that came on between 6-8 pm. I only say that to show you that there's no escaping time. Occasionally, you'll hear

someone talk about them needing to be awakened by the alarm. Everything we do in life has to deal with time. Allow me to speak to the people who have jobs. Can you not say they, too, have to deal with time because they must clock in and out?

Throughout your reading of this chapter and throughout this book, you'll need time to finish it, or anything for that matter. Time is a noun. Time is merely the temporary length of an event or entity's existence.

The instrument used to spread this word is only because time was granted to me.

Surely you've heard the expression about someone saying they haven't seen you since many moons ago.

All I'm doing is shedding light on the things we already know. Not realizing how long it takes to write this down and then type it out is time permitted. Patience can be a virtue or a hindrance if you fail to understand it. I still recall my Granny telling me to be in the house before the sun and the lights come on.

It would help if you understood that night and day fall under time. Don't be alarmed, as I know most of this stuff you already know; I'm writing to inform you that it's something to consider. When you can put it all together, God can use you in the best way possible.

You must first learn the process to benefit from the progress. **T.I.M.E.**, to me, is the acronym for **"TRANSITIONING. INTO. MOMENTS. ETERNITY."** We spend our entire life trying to figure out our purpose in the lie. The problem with that is time is only sometimes permitted to us. Only God can give you the time to do anything and everything. I am very grateful for this time that God has allotted me.

The distance that it takes to get from your house to work is within time again. When the sun rises, and the moon comes up would also be relevant to time. As I look at my birth certificate, there's also the date and time. I did childish things as a child, but as time passed, I grew into a young man. From there, I transitioned into becoming the king God intended me to be.

Yet, it was all in God's timing.

We, as spiritual beings, can only grasp the importance of time once we experience a tragedy, emergency, or something specific.

How conscious are you when it comes to other people's time? How do you measure the time that's beneficial to you? How would you feel if you didn't have time in the day, month, or year? What examples of your life do you wish you had more time to deal with whatever was taking place?

Even as I write this chapter, I think of my publisher and how she's always on me about punctuality! To my credit, though, I'm not trying to write a book for now. I hope the Illustration of my mind to pen and pad will be timeless. The tempo of a song and the pulse in my heartbeat are also relevant to time. There may have been a long interval between me understanding who I am as a king, but I wouldn't change that enduring stretch that God put me on because that's where the wisdom, knowledge, and understanding stem from.

Being a Doer of the Word taught me that anything can be achieved by putting the Creator of Time first. There's nothing unique about me or anything I'm relaying to you. The only thing that matters is that God uses me to help you get a better understanding through my life experiences about time, hoping that you may take heed to better your efforts as it relates to time because I can assure you this. You're born to die.

My definition of time is what God gave me; its acronym is **"TRANSITIONING INTO MOMENTS ETERNITY"** Don't waste it.

Stepping inside the restroom just now, I know what must be done. Deadlines are the exact thing as time. How long does it take to bake a cake? When you process what time means and stands for. It will improve you in all the areas of your life you may have been struggling with.

One Mississippi. Two Mississippi, all still relevant to the time. These are the seconds that I'm sacrificing to break down the understanding of time to assist everyone else so that they may also save time.

There's no way I am the only person who wishes they had a few more seconds on the clock for their favorite team in sports because it would've given them the championship, we all need, desire, and treasure, just as we do the air we breathe.

There have been many disappointments because of the lack of time or how we tend to abuse it. Time is patience. Ask any woman who's about to go shopping or needs to get her hair and nails done. Rest assured that there's not enough time in a day for them, when it comes to those things.

These things are essential to women, but more importantly, it's the time because they wouldn't be able to without it.

Time management is something that we must put as a priority. We must become Master of It. It's the one thing that I emphasize to you the most.

Allow me to elaborate a little deeper.

I'd like for you to know that there's nobody in this world who isn't equal. So, when I say this, what I mean is that you, me, Warren Buffett, Elon Musk, Jeff Bezos, Sam Walton, Jay Z, Donald Trump, Kanye West, Oprah, Beyonce or anyone who's in the top 1 percent. We all have the same thing in common and that's, we all have the same amount of time in the day. The only difference between the wealthiest people on the planet and the not so wealthy, is how they utilize and manage their time. They're not wasting it by not producing or having negative thoughts. They are using their time to ensure that they're always progressing to the next venture and into the future, by focusing on the future.

When the expiration of life comes, that's because there's a deadline for all things in life. We are born to die, so time is everlasting only to time itself.

How selfish was it to think that I was special enough not to thank God for it when I wasn't genuinely appreciative of it, when I lost something that wasn't worth the time.

I'd rather bear my soul and allow time to elapse if I knew there's a benefit for someone other than myself. That's my greatest gift in life. It's the ability to save people time. I've always been known to do for others. It's what my Granny instilled in me. A sacrificing of my time to give others more of it, is no different than what the Father's Son did for us to be able to be sinful and live the life that we live by sacrificing His time.

Now, in no way am I saying that I'm Him. With the wisdom I've acquired in my many years of living. I know and respect time in a different light than most.

The challenge we all face is that time gives nobody in this world an indication of when it shows up for good or bad. I say that with confidence because nobody in this world has it to waste, and when mistakes are made, then time is wasted because we must go back and fix it or take the chance of something being incomplete.

This chapter and the book will give you something to think about. What and How I choose to use my time is my prerogative. Well, at this instance in life. I choose to use it to bless others. That is what time is to me. **Transitioning Into Moments Eternity**.

Allow time to exist, just as the Creator does. Measure your time to maximize your time. I only hope that the time you took from your life, was worth you reading this chapter and book. With great pride, I'd like to thank everyone who gave their time before me to have the freedom to write this book.

I thank the Holy Spirit for my time with my mother, when daughters and sons don't; but to take this blessing for granted, God has blessed me not to be so hypocritical. I thank God for my time with my children when others don't get to be with theirs. Hopefully, the insight that God has given me to write this chapter will guide you in a way that will save you time to do whatever it is that you may need it for.

Take time to tell that person you're sorry or you love them. Kiss your significant other before leaving the house, for it may be the last time you have to do so. Hug your children as if tomorrow was your last chance to see them because we never know when we will have to do so.

I only wish that time becomes a priority in your life before it's too late. Open your heart to these words if they apply to you and take heed if they don't.

~DEEPEST THOUGHTS~

1. How is your time best used?

2. Who would you give your time to?

3. What about this chapter can you apply to your life?

4. What did you gain from reading this chapter and could you benefit from it?

~Chapter 9~

THREE POINTING BACK

Always remember that when you point the finger at someone or something, you have three pointing back at you. The judgment within us is what we do consistently without being aware we are.

What type of being would I be if I asked someone to do something but wouldn't do it in return?

The power of those three words, put together, puts you in a position where you're either being honest with yourself or nothing good is happening within your brain. Instead, we're talking about a person's looks, how they talk, or what they smell like.

The moment you decide to speak of anything that isn't good. That's when you're being judgmental and pointing fingers, but remember that you have three pointing back. That's one of the reasons why I chose to write this book. Speaking my truth, by being entirely and wholeheartedly honest with myself, will allow me to be honest with everyone else. It also puts anyone who thinks they know me into a category where they will point the finger or only speak kind words when it comes to me.

This book of honesty will only take away the ability to say anything negative about me because I'm already enlightening the world about the good, the bad, and the ugly about my past, my present, and the near future, God willing.

When people realize that I'm the author of this book, they'll say and do anything to make me look bad by trying to discredit me and assassinate my character.

You'd be amazed how many people would love to see me fail, but who am I as it relates to people in this world? Some people have been through worse and will go through worse than anything I can imagine.

Let's look at the world; it's always something behind you. Most of the time, people speak negatively about or judge you. It sets you off in a direction or having to explain yourself.

How would you, or anyone for that matter, respond to someone that's being hypocritical? Why would anyone desire to tear down another human being when we wouldn't want those things to happen to us? How

often have you had a dispute with someone that's being judgmental or pointing the finger at you?
When individuals are pointing the finger at you, most likely, you're acknowledging or accepting what they're saying, or it'll lead to a dispute that's not even worthy because they're speaking about everyone other than themselves, which is why it's entitled, three pointing back.
So, allow me to echo these things about pointing fingers. Karma is one of the things that will happen to you no matter what. I recall numerous occasions in my way of living, without regard for how others felt about their situations.

So fast forward to when I'm trying to change my life, the things you once did are now being done to you? What you put out of your mind, body, and soul will surely boomerang back to you at some point of time in your life. I'm only here to inform anyone reading this, hoping that the journey God has me on, you'd be better equipped to understand how to deal with life situations as they come with everything that has happened to me in my lifetime that wasn't good.

I have to ask myself what I did to warrant this; most likely, it's because I did it in my past to someone. The hell of the storm that we go through in life are the ones that we create.

We are the masters of our fate in every way. We must look at ourselves when we're looking for a change. What if I was walking down the street or in the mall and I saw this lady or man, and in my mind, I'm saying how ugly they may be or how badly dressed they are?

Well, that's me pointing out someone else flaws when Lord knows; I wouldn't want anyone thinking or speaking about my flaws. Only God can judge me and everyone in this world. My question to my audience would be. Why are we playing God?

Physical characteristics about us as a race will always be a topic for people to point the finger at. What is it about deformity that gives people the right to speak about that human being?

How would you feel if you were pregnant with a child who grew up with some disability? The child is born into sin.

In what ways is it fair to that child to be treated as such? Racism in this world would be the same; simply because my skin color isn't the same as yours, you'd feel the need to downplay me and the culture.

What if someone was born into a different race than what they were? How would you feel if your Mother, Father, children, and anyone you love had to experience what we as a race had to deal with?

Would you feel comfortable with them speaking about you in that way?

Growing up, I've had the finger pointed at me because of my height; instead, it's from my relatives or children from my neighborhood.

I was picked on in elementary school because I only had one pair of pants and a shirt with my shoes from Dollar General. Even when I got something new, it needed to be better than those with more.

Imagine your child wanting to take their life because they've been bullied early on. We never know how someone else may react to the criticism that they're putting out there.

You may point the finger at them, but I can guarantee it's more being pointed back at you. Point the finger and tell me what you see.

As I was raised up in the deep south, I remember this little kid with bumps all over his face, so I always thought I was ugly, and it didn't help that I received the most criticism from my family. Even as I grew up, I always was mindful of being judgmental towards others because of what I had to endure, so I never wanted that energy to come back at me. Worldly things are also grounds for people to point the finger at you. It could be that beautiful lady that caught your attention, or it could be a young man. Would you treat me differently because I didn't drive the vehicle that made them feel and look great? What if they viewed you differently than you viewed yourself?

Well, that is also pointing the finger, and rest assured your day of having it done to you will soon follow. When people point, they fail to grasp they're indicating something that isn't a reality. How dare you or anyone who may insinuate anything about me that isn't in the best light.

Accepting the truth when it's being brought to light isn't being judgmental or pointing the finger. It's merely an observation about the opinion that someone may have that can be a blessing to and for you. When you point out, have you thought about what something is? Have you ever asked yourself if you were in the other person's shoes at which you're pointing the finger? How often are we critical of an athlete or entertainer?

Are we that harsh on a player making a game-winning field goal or basket? Put yourself in that person's shoes and imagine someone pointing the finger at your mother, sister, or daughter. If it were easy, more people would be doing it as well.

What would you do to ensure that it doesn't happen? Well, as for me. I'd make sure that I wasn't pointing the finger. I'd treat that individual how I would like to be treated to ensure that energy or karma doesn't come back to haunt me or whoever is on the opposite side of the finger-pointing.

Allow your brain to travel with me to a better mindset. I'm no expert, nor am I God, but what I am is an example of how to be in life.

Can you imagine if you had only one leg, one arm? How would you feel if someone pointed the finger and laughed at you?

How would that make you feel? What wave of emotions would you believe you'd experience if, for some reason, growing up, your peers knew that you used to wet the bed, and they all started calling you pee-body? How do you think that person felt you were talking about and pointing the finger at their flaws? We all have flaws; nobody in this world is perfect but the Creator of life. As I write this, the reader will have something to say, but at that moment, they are making my case about three pointing back about what I'm referencing and about to say.

Most Christians will be the first to point the finger at what I'm about to write, but my level of understanding and opinion is precisely what it is.

It's my God-giving choice to be a DOER OF THE WORD. I'm speaking about those people in the L.G.B.T.Q. Community.

Can you imagine what they have to deal with in this world that we live in?

So according to the word of God. It states that only God can judge you.

It also mentions that without sin, he can cast the first stone. Last but not least, is the one that comes up that the Creator's Son died on the cross for our sins, even though it states things about having sex with the same gender. I can't speak for anyone else, but I and my understanding is that you can't take one piece of the Bible and not take the other. I mean, do you genuinely believe that sin is a sin? So, if the Creator's Son died on the cross for all our sins, how can anyone point the finger at someone being gay? How can we pick the speck out of someone else's eye when we have a flaw the size of a Cadillac on our own? We live in this world that judges, but we don't want to be the judge, and as someone who's been on both sides of the spectrum.

It's not as pleasant to be on the side where you're being judged because karma is coming back around, but how you handle it will determine everything.

Allow this chapter to enlighten you about our sins and point that finger at ourselves, and when that takes place is when this world will become the place that God intended it to be. Nobody can force you to accept our wrongdoing, so we must make the change. Make the change to better yourself.

Do not be judgmental, and you won't be judged. Spread love into the universe, so the better you've sown into the world may circle back to you. Doing these things empowers your mind to become more than you'd ever hoped for.

It's the one thing God had hoped we would someday understand: not to be judgmental.

Am I wrong to say these things, hoping they could someday come to pass? My love for humanity will only be shown to me when I learn to be what I preach rather than being of this world and pointing the finger. Remember that when you point the finger, you MUST BE GOD, BECAUSE ONLY GOD CAN!!!

~NOTES~

~DEEPEST THOUGHTS~

1. Have you ever pointed the finger at someone and if so, why did you?

2. What was the benefit of pointing the finger?

3. Is pointing the finger the same as judging?

4. Would you desire to be judged by anyone or anything that isn't God?

5. What about this chapter gave you something to think about?

6. How would this chapter benefit you after reading it?

~Chapter 10~

A.S.K.
(ASK. SEEK. KNOCK)

How ironic that the first letter of the alphabet starts with the letter "A." The irony is that asking for something starts with the letter "A." What's the significance of it all? Well, it's the fact that asking for something starts from within. God has repeatedly poured His blessings into us all, but it starts from the spiritual being that we are.

We must remove the fleshly way of thinking to gain what we're asking for. Questions directed towards someone can also be the same as asking for something. Are we better than God that we don't need help?

As I continue this journey, I understand I may be put through the wringer. When you ask the Creator for patience, guidance, love, or anything else, know it's not given to you. You're put into certain situations to develop those attributes, as I recall what I asked the Holy Spirit for. I am in awe because everything I've asked for was given to me, not in my time, but in God's time. We should be cautious of what we're asking for because it happens when we speak.

What is it that you're asking for?

Have you found yourself on the receiving end of anything, whether positive or negative? In case you didn't know or understand. When someone gives you the third degree, they ask for something to happen. Hopefully, what I'm speaking of will resonate with you and have you heed what's to follow, and let's be honest. Those words are the same as taking action.

Allow me to elaborate on requesting things from the God above. I recall requesting to be one of the greatest prophets besides His Son. When I asked for those things in life, I did so wholeheartedly without a shadow of a doubt. When you apply those things to words, a certain level of comfort comes over you, turning into reality. How about when I was locked up and had to be interrogated? I'm only speaking about things as it relates to A.S.K.

What about when the mother uses the word to ask their children to do something? What about the people that are married? Nobody could be in that position if they couldn't ask. Nobody should be prideful about asking for things that are needed versus what you want. When you ask for things, sometimes it happens in a blink of an eye, and sometimes it requires patience.

Would you be patient for the things you need that can be of assistance, or would you be hasty for a short-term gain but with long-term pain?

How often do you recall asking for something only to be told no? Well, "NO" only means the **"NEXT OPPORTUNITY"** to me.

We should grasp what we're asking for and be ready for what we're asking. What time of day would also fall beneath the question of asking? What must be done to get the answer when someone doesn't know your age or height? The question must be asked.

Indeed, you've experienced someone prying into your business, even if you didn't want them to, but make no mistakes about it.

That, too, would require them to ask the question. I would be lying to myself if I said that I've never asked for anything in my life, but it's also my responsibility to go after whatever I'm asking for, and the thing I asked for is to be truthful.

As a father, a son, and a grandson, among many other things, I can't say that I've never asked for anything. I know there's only one who's always answered me when I needed answers, and that's G.O.D.!

You may recall earlier a few chapters back about me being bullied. Well, even then, I had to ask God to assist me to help end the psychological bullying effect; having that happen to me is part of why I'm in this position. It set me on a path I could never have envisioned, but as I think about my life growing up, I've always asked God to be the best humanitarian ever to have existed. Now, as a child growing up, we tend to throw tantrums when things don't come when we want them, but as the good book states, He is our shepherd, and we shall not want.

So, we must learn not to get in God's way when we ask for things so He can deliver whatever we need. We must always allow the Holy Spirit to do the job we ask for if we're ever to move forward in the most positive way as a human race, even though there's work to do after we ask for it. Whatever it is that you're seeking is hidden from us. Most of us who know the purpose of life will also value the quest that God has us on. All those things align with faith, but how would you know without understanding?

For many years I used to chase after the wrong things. I would be after the worldly things in life, which led me down the wrong road because I ignored the real and answered to the fake.

Have you ever shunned away from the truth? Why do we neglect the things that could benefit us? Can you say righteousness should be neglected? I, for one, would rather sniff out the spiritual gifts that God has put inside us.

I'm tracking down the spiritual truth to lead my mind out of the darkness it once was in. Do you remember the game called hide and seek? This is the asking of the hiding part, and because of the lack of understanding that some of you may have, allow me to elaborate.

The seeking is the action part of things. It's similar to faith without works is dead deeds. Do you believe everyone on this journey of spirituality was given everything? I think not. The answers to life can be right before you, yet so far. As a grown individual, I can attest that lessons had to be learned to appreciate the finer things in life better. I repeatedly asked myself why I must be after the things that cost me the most important thing: time. The best advice I can give you would be to search for your purpose, for that endeavor will most likely surprise you out of the oblivion you're inside. Never give up seeking true love. Don't stop seeking honor. Indulge your very existence into moving forward. Keep your eyes focused ahead of you rather than looking back. Go gunning for whatever it is that you've set your mind to.

You can be sure that your life will be full of trials and tribulations.

Being alive will have its challenges, which you'll face. But the unseen thing will ensure you make it to the other side of eternity because that's all death is. It's simply passing through time into eternity.

Wherever you're at in life, good or bad, I'm here to tell you that life goes on. Don't get caught up in the things left behind you when your spirit travels throughout the universe. We're all just frequencies put together to form this energy of life that we're living in.

In my years of living thus far. I've continued to beat the bushes, searching for the light, not knowing it's within.

Analyze this. Imagine the quarterback of an NFL team goes back to throw a pass. As he's doing so, there are many variables he must factor in to be able to either get the yardage needed or be able to throw a touchdown and win on one throw.

He must keep his eyes downfield while paying attention to the edge rusher coming at him from both ends or his right side or blind side.

Let's remember the interior linemen who would also be coming at him. Those are just a few obstacles he must look for, having only seconds to execute his feature. He must do this over and over again.

What does this have to do with seeking? Are you wondering? Well, it's quite simple.

The wide receiver he's throwing the ball to must move forward to seek out where the ball will be thrown to catch the ball to gain the first down or the game-winning touchdown.

He, too, will face defenders and obstacles trying to catch the pigskin material shaped into what we call a football. To gain what they are searching for, they must keep their eyes downfield while being aware of using their peripheral information about their surroundings. I say this because when we're searching for things or seeking the stuff that would complete us.

We, too, must understand that we will face obstacles and challenges while seeking progression. We have to adapt to our surroundings and keep track of time. I can be the first to attest that many people will face a difficult decision while seeking a better life than you or I may have.

If I could pass along anything that would help you along the way, it would be for you to trust God. Trust the God in you, for the Holy Spirit is stronger than your flesh. Train your mind to see the light at the end of the tunnel to whatever your goal is.

As long as you don't give up on yourself and demonstrate faith, I can say that no matter what, God will grant you the pleasure of relishing in joy for seeking the desired thing.

Knock, knock. Who is it? Have you ever heard of that game before? A question follows up as a matter of fact. A sequence of things happens before the setup can be complete. It's no different in this chapter.

First, there's the Ask; next, it was about seeking, which has us here.

I can't make anyone walk through the door once it opens. You must be mindful about what doors you're asking to be opened because when done so with complete conviction, that's the moment it happens.

You have yet to deny the delivery driver of the pizza you requested, nor have you rejected the person from the U.P.S. that's bringing that purse or shoes you've ordered.

What about those times when you were in college and needed a certain grade to be able to pass, which would give you the total credits needed?

The point that I'm trying to make. You're asking for things, seeking to obtain them, and then walking through the door to receive them.

Everything asked for before seeing it would be the same as demonstrating faith. I'm only trying to have you expand your mind by eliminating the doubt. Remember the importance of the power of knocking and what you gain from the knock or the person who's doing the knocking.

As a mother, would you permit your children into your bedroom when it's inappropriate? Do you give up when someone closes the door on you after you've given it your all at an interview? These things are all important in how we move in life. They are essential to brain functionality. Food for thought. Please pay attention to that friend or relative that comes to you knowing they're not in their best state of mind asking you for things.

Always remember that they open the moment you ask for them to be opened.

You also have to keep in mind when to close the door in the time when someone is knocking. All these things will be achieved when you have reached a certain level of understanding. Trust me when I tell you. I did not get here overnight. It took years of me asking, seeking, and knocking.

The character was being built without me ever knowing it. Resilience was being trained; instead, I knew it. When

the understanding of knowing that the door swings both ways. I then knew how to walk into my purpose.
Continue knocking down doors on anything that you believe in. Ask for what you need in life when it's for the right reasons.
Always seek out what's important to you. I can only speak for myself when I say that I've applied those things I'm writing about to my everyday life, which brought me to this conclusion.

Of course, some people will speak against anything I'm writing. That's also proving my point about how the world is a hypocrite. I'm hoping for my faith in humanity. I believe in the Holy Spirit that I can be used in a way that will only bring peace. I pray that unity will be placed in

We all need oxygen to breathe. We also know that we need trees to produce that. What happens when there are no longer enough trees to produce oxygen for the number of people on this planet? I say that because if we keep knocking on the door of trying to play God, we'll soon find ourselves in the position to be just that, but not having the power and understanding to do so.

Is that not "SOMETHING TO THINK ABOUT?"

~DEEPEST THOUGHTS~

1. What are you asking for in life that benefits you?

2. What are you seeking to be and get out of life?

3. When do you believe it's time to start knocking for the things you deserve in life?

4. Are you asking the right questions or the right people for what it is that you're in search of?

~NOTES~

PUBLISHING HOUSE, LLC.

THIS BOOK WAS PUBLISHED BY VJ PUBLISHINGHOUSE, LLC.

For further information contact us via email at: vjpublishinghouse@gmail.com

Visit our website at: www.Vjpublishinghouse.com Write us at:

20451 NW 2nd Avenue Suite 112 Miami
Gardens, Florida 33169

Where Your Stories Are Built On A Solid Foundation

www.ingramcontent.com/pod-product-compliance
Lightning Source LLC
Chambersburg PA
CBHW032051090426
42744CB00004B/164

* 9 7 8 1 9 3 9 2 3 6 1 5 9 *